Maureen

Your Intuition
Handbook

How to
DEPEND ON YOU!

The Awakened Press

The Awakened Press
www.theawakenedpress.com

The Awakened Press

Cover Illustration by Agsandrew from Dreamstime.com

Cover Design by David Moratto

Interior Design by Fabricio P. 7

Ornament Divider Image by Freepik.com (interior design)

First edition.

ISBN: 978-1-989134-10-8

Intuition guides us along to our destiny if we allow it to. We simply need to acknowledge and feel the loving connection we have with our soul.

I offer this book with my heartfelt wish to inspire and encourage others to trust and believe in themselves and to recognize their "authentic self".

I also wish to help people save a lot of their precious time from having to constantly question themselves by over-thinking; wondering if they should have or could have done things a different way.

I am honoured to be able to deliver messages and insights that can bring clarity and understanding, and to acknowledge that it is our birthright to have access to our OWN information. I dedicate this book to all people who have the courage to SIMPLY BE YOU!

—Maureen Freeman, SAGE

Contents

Foreword

Over the past twenty-five years of being a professional intuitive reader, I have been asked numerous times when and how I knew I was psychic, and if I have written a book to explain how to connect with our intuition.

Besides doing thousands of readings, I have written and published many articles and channeled writings, done lectures, and held classes on developing one's psychic abilities. Over time I have experimented with many various teachings, techniques and practices in self-discovery. I also explored and discovered many of my own. I have taken what resonated with me and decided it was time to share my findings, with the intention of encouraging and supporting others in discovering and connecting with their own inner voice, their intuition.

So here it is: *Your Intuition Handbook*. Let me take you by the hand to show you how valuable and magical it is to connect with your intuition, enhancing your journey called life, and to have a better understanding of life itself.

Being the age I am now and looking back at my life, I am able to see the tapestry I have woven. Some were beautiful, magical, easy threads and others were difficult threads that were challenging yet valuable, which I see now. All needed to be experienced to show me and assist me in being who I am. We don't always see that from a linear place when we are "in it". And yes, at times I took diversions when not paying attention to my inner voice. That is the human part of us. But somehow you get back on track and realize it's simpler to listen to that inner voice as it is your *soul's whisper*, there to guide you on your way to navigate through your experiences in your life and show you who you are.

We live in a beautiful dimension visually but day to day can be most challenging and hard to understand. Due to humans being "exactly the same yet completely different", it is often difficult to communicate or fathom what goes on here. I feel if we have a better understanding of who we are and how we can connect here and beyond this Earth plane, it can assist us and bring some understanding during our lifetimes.

We are in a very changing world and it is a momentous time in the history of planet Earth. Being able to listen to your own guidance—your intuition—will help you to interpret what is occurring, which is of the utmost importance for our future on Earth. That is another reason why I felt so compelled to write this book: to encourage people to trust and believe in themselves and to shine their authentic selves, and to know how important that is for the good of ALL.

As you experience this book I hope to save you a lot of time questioning yourself. This is my wish to everybody—to see that you have access to your own information. To recognize within yourself that you have this innate power that is the essence of who you are.

Wouldn't it be wonderful to recognize and communicate with everyone you meet from soul to soul, essence to essence? Then there would be truth, love, peace, harmony and FREEDOM!

Our lives are meant to be a collective contribution, not a competition. I once read a statement by an anonymous person, "Life is an experience to be lived, not a problem to be solved." I agree!

So let's get started and explore what intuition is and how to connect with it.

—Maureen Freeman, SAGE

Intuition

What Is Intuition?

If you looked it up in a dictionary it would define intuition as "perceived by immediate insight, immediate apprehension without reason."

Some refer to intuition as our "sixth sense". I refer to intuition as *the voice of your spirit within*.

I have always known of this inner voice since being a child. I didn't talk about it then, I just assumed everyone heard it. As I got older I realized that isn't so. My connection increased and altered somewhat, but those stories are for another book, another time!

Everyone has intuition, we just need to recognize it. This voice is invisible and "silent" which is an oxymoron, as our physical voice can be heard. It comes through as a strong *knowing*. This silent voice is so important; it is our "spirit/soul" and our connection to the Life Force Energy or Universal Energy, that of All That Is. Some prefer to use the word God or Source.

For myself, I had to get past thinking the words "soul" and "spirit" means you are religious. Same with the word "God". I realized it does not have to be religious; it is our *essence self*; the *essence of who you are*. You can have your own perception of what they mean; it is about how you feel using the words. Just choose whatever word that resonates with you and you feel comfortable with.

To further connect with your intuition, I suggest to perceive yourself as a spirit with a body, rather than a body with a spirit. Why would that matter? You are placing the emphasis on your spirit, firstly. They are equally important, but we identify with our physical body as we see it with our physical eyes. By placing the focus on your spirit firstly, you can sense that your spirit/soul is energy that has an amazing intricate body that houses it to experience life on Earth. It is an eternal energy that still lives on after leaving this Earth plane.

I have found that the more I relate to being energy, the more I realize our capacity and ability to communicate with and experience the invisible.

Your soul/spirit is like your hard drive that holds all the information about you. It knows what lessons you are here for and it knows the perfect timing of your blossoming, in alignment and accordance with those lessons. It is most important to form a strong bond and relationship with your soul/spirit. You will then hear its voice. *It is the most important relationship in your life!* Your spirit is your compass throughout your life, if you allow it to be.

So let me take you by the hand and show you how tuning in to your intuition will help you enhance your life!

Tuning in to Your Intuition Helps You Because…

You Can Depend on YOU!

There is no shadow of a doubt that when you pay attention and listen to your intuition you have less stress and anxiety as you are not having to question and analyze everything that is happening in your life. You can be more spontaneous and not feel you have to plan, control, or worry about the future. You can "be in the moment." When you understand how it works and as you learn to listen and accept what you hear, you are taking the pressure off of yourself by not thinking you have to come up with the right answers all the time.

This is not to say that every moment of the day will be wonderful and that you won't have challenges. However, by acknowledging its guidance, you know that whatever you are experiencing is what you are meant to, now. Your perception changes from classifying your experiences as "good", "bad", "right" or "wrong"; *they just are*. Some are lovely experiences, some are challenging.

This is not to say that some people have experiences out of their control, where they are not able to listen to their inner voice to help themselves; or the situation they are in is restricting so they cannot make their own choices. Some people's lives seem to be blessed where another person's life seems to have challenge after challenge, struggle after struggle. It is hard not to compare one to another. When we do though, we are doing so without knowing the essence of those lives. Many factors are involved beyond what we can ever perceive. That is why it is much simpler to be accepting of what is. There are many storylines to each and every soul on this planet.

Your soul is not going to guide you in the wrong direction even though what you are experiencing may seem wrong to you. Many people think if something is difficult or challenging, then they must have taken a wrong turn. Not so! Some of the most challenging experiences are our greatest gifts. Sometimes, if not all the time, the obstacle is the perfect path.

Trusting Your Intuition

Your intuition is a part of you that you can trust. It's fast (when you're in tune) it's *free* and it is reliable! You can make choices in your life yourself, as the true you (inner you/soul) is the only one that knows exactly what is right for you. You can intuitively know what to do in any given situation.

When you trust your intuition you can make decisions (day to day little ones and more serious ones) that go beyond logic. Sometimes it may seem strange with what you are hearing or feeling to do, but you find out by following through that it was perfect. You "feel" what is right for you, not what you "think".

There are many oxymorons and illusions in this dimension on Earth. The "unknown" is actually "the known" as your soul "knows" how your journey is to unfold if you accept and allow it to and follow its guidance.

Being connected with your intuition also keeps you "alerted" to stay out of harm's way. When you pay attention to your intuition, and you get a strong feeling not to do something or go somewhere at that moment, there are reasons why that you may not know then, but it may be revealed to you later in time. Simply trusting it and following through is what is important when you get the "hit", not the reason. (We will talk more about intuition and timing later on in this book.)

Being in tune with your intuition can be most helpful to you in an awkward situation such as a power outage or a natural disaster when there is no way to communicate physically. You can tune in to sense what to do, and to feel whether your loved ones are OK.

Your intuition helps in all relationships—especially loved ones, partners, children, and your pets. You can sense and feel them and their needs and how they are, without words. You can communicate silently by "tuning in".

When you continue to listen to your intuition, you then realize how self-sufficient you have become. You find that you are not "needy". In other words, you are able to trust yourself in making choices in your life, rather than having someone else make them for you or the need to always depend on another to help you.

You also begin to sense the connection to an energy beyond this Earth plane that feels benevolent; the Universal Energy of All That Is; Source or God Force Energy. It is an expanded awareness where you feel and just know that there is much more to existence than here on Earth.

Your intuition is your connection to navigate in this 3D world but on a different channel. When you realize this, it changes your whole experience of being here. It's magical! It is operating on two channels at once. You are then embracing your humanness, your body/mind; and your divinity, your spirit/ soul; Human and Spirit functioning simultaneously!

You feel more engaged knowing there is much more to being here on Earth and you can feel passion to expose and share who you are and your gifts and talents in contributing to creating a peaceful world. This may be something as simple as just being kind and peaceful within your life. You find you don't relate to the drama that can be created by humans, which is pure ego and "fake power". The ego is fear-based and does not serve for the highest good for ALL. When you connect with your soul and listen to its guidance you can detach from this drama and "simply be you".

What you are looking to achieve is to integrate body, mind, and spirit operating in balance to your full potential. Operating without using your intuition and only being aware of your physical body would be like only using one program on your computer when you have the means to open and connect with another one that assists you in a more complete way with what you are wishing to achieve. Being aware of this is exciting to see what is presented to you. Your blueprint unfolds as you experience your life that is your own unique journey.

How Does Your Intuition Help You?

We live in a world where we are exposed to so much information through technology, it can be overwhelming. It can make you feel so confused, you don't know what to believe is true. There are almost too many choices and extremes, and I feel many people have anxiety due to this. For instance, you are reading it's best to eat certain foods that are supposedly good for you, and there are lists of all the foods you shouldn't eat. If you are able to listen to your intuition, as you are reading this, you can sense which suggestions resonate within you and which ones don't. Listening to your intuition lets you know if it's a "yes" or "no" for you, despite what experts say. This is also true for other suggestions you may read. Even though we appear to be exactly the same, we are all unique and completely different!

You can probably recall many times where you had a feeling come through to do something a different way, but you ignored it by doing it the way you normally would.

As an example:

You always go the same way to get to work. It is basically automatic; you are so used to repeating it daily. One day you are feeling you shouldn't go the usual way but you ignore it and continue on your usual route. As you do so, you are suddenly stopped and find yourself in a huge traffic jam. You can't see why, but find you are delayed for half an hour. Feeling anxious, you are mad at yourself for not listening to that inner voice telling you to take a different route. You arrive super late to work and have missed the meeting that was important for you.

Here is an example of when you do listen to your inner voice:

Let's say you find yourself looking for a job. Three interviews show up and each one offers you a position. One is so much money it seems like why not just say yes to it, even though it's not really what you'd like. The second one is much less money but you like the position offered. The third offers good money and is a position you would feel good about, but it's a lot of travelling time to and fro, which presents you may wish to move if you took that one.

You think about all of your options from a linear, logical, practical perspective, checking the pros and cons of each one.

People are telling you that you should take the one that pays the best. You hear them, but since you have been practising listening to your intuitive voice, you sit quietly by yourself and feel each position to sense what is best for you.

You ask from within "what is the highest and best" for you at this point in your life. You sense the one where you have to travel quite a distance back and forth. You are somewhat surprised at the answer but trust to accept that position. You feel apprehensive about it, but the feeling from within is strong so you trust its guidance. You also check in with yourself to feel if you should move. You hear and sense not right away. So you trust that and take the job and commute. During the first month of learning your new job and getting used to it, a colleague asks you if you know of anyone who would want to rent a lovely apartment that their friend has for rent. She describes it and it turns out it has everything you would want! You look at it, love it and move in.

As you continue working and enjoying your new job and your apartment, you meet another colleague that started after you. You become friends outside of work and she introduces you to some of her friends. You meet a man who made your heart skip a beat in the first second you had eye contact! He feels the same way about you; you eventually marry and have the family you always wished for!

Your soul knew you were to take the job and you listened to its voice rather than be tempted by money or settling for a job that would be boring. Look at how listening to your intuition directed your life. You feel grateful you listened to yourself rather than listening to others as they were trying to persuade you to take the one with the highest money offer.

Listening to your intuition gives you some freedom from worrying, wondering, wishing, and wanting things to be different. It "takes the monkey off your back" from always questioning and analyzing whether you are doing "it" right and making the right decisions. It saves you from being too hard on yourself or thinking you made the wrong choice when things turned out differently than you thought it would; yet the outcome was not wrong, it was exactly right. You don't perceive changes as "failures" and the need to defend yourself. You are accepting of the way it is.

You may find that when you begin to empower yourself by recognizing your soul and listening to its voice, some people will not be able to relate to you as you seem different. People may think you are being arrogant or better than them, even though this is not so. You have decided to make your own decisions in life, by trusting yourself and how you feel. As you become stronger in yourself, you may find that some people snub you or don't want to associate with you. This happens as you have something they want, even though they may not realize this. *This only happens with people that are not "in tune" with themselves.* Others that are "in tune" will be attracted to you as they recognize you are on the same wavelength.

As you see by the benefits written above and by the examples given, intuition can help you in so many ways.

What Blocks Intuition?

Some people find it mysterious or are hesitant about their intuition or "tuning in" to themselves due to not knowing what it truly is. Some see it as religious by using the words "spirit" or "soul". Some are fearful it may be evil or scary, or even a cult.

Some people can't fathom it as they expect to have tangible proof; something they can read or see with the physical eyes. It can't be "seen"; you have to "sense" or "feel" it. If you try to intellectualize it, you will become frustrated as it is not on that channel! There is little to no current scientific explanation such as there is about our other physical five senses.

Some people get confused about how to access it by simply misunderstanding what it is. Some find it difficult to decipher as they feel the need to "think" it. This can come from being programmed to believe it doesn't exist; believing you have no awareness within oneself.

Fear

Fear is mostly what keeps us from being in touch and trusting our intuition, in addition to not being taught you have it or knowing what it is. We have all been conditioned and controlled through various experiences in our lives—from family, teachers, society, and religion, just to name a few. Our minds contain a lot of "programming" that no longer serves us or perhaps never did—that we need to let go of to have clarity. When one lives in fear, which is a lower vibration, it can block the passion for life itself. It limits and restricts you. Overcoming fear removes blocks so you can then explore new interests and feel fulfilled and confident in all you do.

Feeling Unsafe

Some people feel unsafe or too vulnerable to expose who they truly are. They fear ridicule, humiliation, and judgment. This may stem from how they have been treated, from being very sensitive, or if they lack self-confidence. They feel too exposed to be themselves, especially when they have heard over and over again that they "don't know anything" or "they are not good enough". Our minds can hold on to thought forms and images that do not serve us for our highest good, and that can be harmful to our well-being. It is difficult to let go of them if you don't know how to delete them, in order to be clear to believe what is true in your own heart and soul.

Conditioning

Many ways that we have been taught or guided are not empowering. For instance, to love yourself and believe in yourself can be perceived that you are "full of yourself" or egotistical. It can be, if it comes from the ego.

Someone operating from their ego is very self-absorbed, constantly needing attention and having their own way, without caring how it appears and how it affects others.

However, when you love yourself from your *soul*, this is a completely different meaning of "loving yourself". It is recognizing who you truly are; respecting, honouring and loving your beautiful soul. You don't feel the need for attention; you hold a silent power from within. You are kind and caring and you appear confident, in somewhat of a mysterious way.

Emotions

Sometimes emotions get in the way. When you are in situations where you react with intense emotions (being upset, angry, in tears, anxious) while trying to make a decision, you are in your own personal drama and are too disruptive with static energy to be open and clear to receive guidance. When you learn to keep your emotions at a more neutral place, you are then able to feel more balanced so you can be clear to receive guidance. It is best to remind yourself to take a deep breath, try and be calm and not react so you can tune in to what to do about your situation.

Here is an example:

Lisa has grown up in a religious family where it is forbidden to go outside the rules and regulations of the church. Reaching her teenage years, she realizes she is not comfortable with the beliefs of the religion. She is afraid to announce this to her family, as she knows the reaction they will have. She has always felt unsafe to speak her mind, or be herself due to knowing what the consequences will be. However, due to being somewhat of an explorer, she decides she wants to venture off on her own and see the world in a different way. She collaborates with a friend with the same circumstances and they come up with a plan to leave their families. Both are eighteen years old. They are a little afraid of leaving, knowing how their family will react but they convince one another it will be OK; they just want to discover their own way and can't wait to "be themselves", which was denied in the home. They feel excited to be adventurous and discover things they'd like to experience that will teach them who they truly are. Both have been fascinated about the world and the universe. They know they have been programmed and conditioned to believe the power is outside of themselves and they needed to abide by the rules when with their families. None of it resonated within them, so they felt there had to be other teachings to explain what life is about. This point of view was never allowed to be discussed in their homes.

They secretly find jobs so they can support themselves, and next a small apartment to live in. They quietly gather a few things from home that they need and leave. Of course their parents discover they are gone, as they did not come home at the curfew time as usual. Both sets of parents find out where they are and demand for them to return home. Emotions fly and words are exchanged that upset the girls and their parents. The parents cannot control the situation due to the girls being "of age" and seen as adults by law. They leave with frustration and feeling disrespected.

The girls have mixed emotions due to what occurred. They did not want to disrespect their parents, but they felt they needed to be true to themselves. They feel empowered by standing their ground!

Eventually, both mothers ask to meet to discuss things. They tell their daughters they understand that they are adults and have choices; however, they are shocked at how they went about it. The girls explain that they felt unsafe to express how they felt as they knew their fathers would be angry and punish them. They all express their love for one another and the girls say they hope one day their fathers would understand.

This example expresses fear, conditioning, feeling unsafe, the need to control, and intense emotions.

You will learn some techniques to help you with your fears, conditioning, and emotions in the following chapters. These practices assist you to "detach, delete and let go" of energy that may be in the way of hearing your intuition in order to receive guidance that is the highest and best for you.

Addiction to Electronics

We are living in a time where there are so many choices of electronic devices to supposedly help us communicate, as well as entertain us. They do help us to a certain degree; however, too much stimulation from using electronic devices such as cell phones, computers, video games, televisions, etc. can be very addictive. They are like "electronic cocaine"!

It is a known fact that some devices are purposely made to be addictive. That is the truth and most people are not aware of it and have been "hooked". Think of how much time you spend on any of these devices. They offer you access to so much information and amusement that you become unaware of how much time you spend on them. They are wonderful in many ways, yet very disruptive in other ways.

I myself am not a technical person, yet I had to learn to become familiar with the various devices to keep up with the times! I can see the value of them and see how much they can assist us in communicating. But, I have also experienced the addiction saying, "Oh, I'll look up just one more thing," or I have experienced a feeling of anxiousness when I have forgotten my cell phone, which really took me by surprise! I lived a long time without having a cell phone and was fine. So, feeling strange not having it with me showed me how much I rely and depend on it!

When you are constantly "on" and find it hard to turn off your phone or stop being connected to the other devices too, you are truly being "wired" to them and it can become an addiction or an obsession. You cannot tune in to your own self if you are constantly connected electronically. You can become too dependent on them for information. It is best to find balance and be "off" so you can be able to "reboot" yourself and switch channels so you can tune in to your own "hotline" to the Universal Energy through listening to your own self, your intuition. You have access to information beyond computers when you realize you can connect to the "Universal Web".

When You Acknowledge Your Intuition

When you don't acknowledge your intuition, you are dismissing it exists. You are ignoring its voice. In turn, you are denying yourself. Some refer to this as "giving your power away" by trusting another's opinion and ignoring yourself, or taking yourself out of the equation completely. You are not giving recognition to your "authentic self".

You feel powerless when you ignore it. You may also feel alone or lonely or empty, even when your life looks good. Through doing readings, I have met many people that wonder what is wrong with them, as they feel like something is missing even though they have a lovely home, family, and lifestyle. At least it appears that way. When I tune in to them, I may say that I sense that they are not able to make their own decisions or do what they wish to from within. I talk about intuition and whether they are aware of it. Some light up and say "yes" and then they suddenly see that is what is missing. Many feel the need to do what everyone else wants them to do and they go along with it and ignore their own needs or wishes.

When you don't trust and listen to your intuition, you may view much of your life as failures when things haven't turned out as you thought they would or should. Many people process their lives through their thoughts, rather than accepting what is by following their inner guidance. Thinking things "went wrong" is not necessarily true, as what you experienced must have been needed for growth.

When another judges or criticizes you, it is their own insecurities coming through. You needn't be affected by it if you are aware of yourself within, and you have the choice to remove yourself from the situation or not give it any energy. In other words, detach and let it go.

When you don't expose yourself from your soul, eventually your "pilot light" can only flicker. You can feel unfulfilled, lonely and unhappy within yourself. Keeping up an image will eventually implode which can bring on illness, loss of family, friends, and depression.

When you operate from your soul, you *nurture* your soul. It is like watering a plant to encourage it to bloom. *Nothing* can change who you are, no matter what is said or done to you.

Your soul's voice cannot be given away. It will always be there for you, patiently waiting to connect with you. It will never give up on you as it IS who you truly are!

There are simple practices to do to help you become more attuned to your soul and in turn to your intuition, which we will explore in the next section.

How to Connect with Your Intuition

We now know what intuition is, and how much it can enhance our lives when we are aware of it and listen to its silent voice. Now we need to learn how magical and valuable it can be to connect with it in order to have it be the guiding light in our lives.

I like to keep things as simple as I can, so let's do so with exploring our intuition and how to connect with it. Let's also make it fun, not work!

The first step is to give it recognition and acknowledge it is there. It is patiently waiting to meet you, help you, and guide you. Allow it to be the *director* of this play called *life*.

The next step is to learn to accept and trust your intuition's subtle silent messages and to sense its pulse. It is often referred to as a *gut feeling* or *heart-knowing*. It is a feeling or sensing. It is not a thought.

There are a number of ways that a *knowing* is described. Some people have shivers or "goosies" up and down their arms or from their head to their toes. Or a shimmering feeling throughout their body. Some have a tingling at the top of their head or all over. Others have a hit or pain in their stomach, yet others hear a telepathic voice. Some just sense a strong pulse or "wave" in their body or solar plexus.

One of my indicators is my left palm of my hand aches. Sometimes my right one does too. I also hear it telepathically (a silent voice, like a whisper). Or I will feel, "I just know." Many people describe "they just know" rather than the sensations mentioned above.

For me it is like having a twin that I can communicate with! It is like operating on two circuits—our human linear channel and our invisible spiritual channel. We need to acknowledge that both exist and know how important both of them are. Our invisible spiritual channel is much like WiFi; you can't see it, but it works and you know it is there!

It is for you to find your own unique communication with your intuition and what your indicator/s are. To do so, take note of the feelings and sensations you are having when you are practising and experiencing your intuition communicating with you. You may find your signals are different than ones I have mentioned, which is perfect for you! You are discovering your own intuitive voice simply by acknowledging it.

As your relationship with your soul is strengthened, your knowing becomes strengthened, and it is as familiar and common as your other senses. As you become more and more used to listening to it, you are *fine-tuning* your circuits. The more you are aware, the more you expand.

You then may become so in tune you can connect psychically where you are clairvoyant (see visions) clairaudient (hear telepathic voices) clairsentient (sense things). You are adding new channels. This can be very exciting. More of this later!

Practices to Enhance Your Intuition

It takes time to become in-tune with your intuition, so think of it as something new you are practising, rather than something you need to work on. "Work" sounds like work; we don't want to relate to it that way!

Start off simply. Play games with everyday things to practise listening to your intuition. When the phone rings, before answering, *intuitively ask* who it is. Say in your mind, "Who is it?" Then see what name shows up. If it is not the name that came to you, that's OK, don't be too hard on yourself. It takes time.

When you are going out and need to find a parking spot, as you are driving "beam up" that you need a parking spot in front of where you need to go. It is amazing how one will suddenly become available as you arrive! If one isn't available don't think you have done something wrong; it's all timing and sometimes there are other factors outside of our control that get in the way. This is just a fun way to practise!

Do this with other situations. Try communicating telepathically (through frequency waves) with someone you want to be in touch with. Don't be surprised if they call you! Remember though, that when you do this it needs to be done with the highest of intentions, not a manipulation or invasion of privacy. For instance, let's say you are attracted to someone and you wish they would be in touch with you, so you want to try to "make" them connect with you. When you do this, it needs to be done with integrity, for the highest and best for all concerned. So rather than trying to "make" someone be in touch, you may word it that you "welcome and would love to hear from them if it's for the highest and best for both." That way you are operating on a different frequency rather than trying to "make" someone do something as that is manipulation. Be mindful of the words you choose to use.

Here is an example:

You meet someone at a coffee shop and become very attracted to them. You smile at one another and he asks you if you'd like to join him. You have a wonderful conversation and realizing the time, you say your goodbyes to hurry off to your appointment. Later on you keep thinking about him; you feel something deeper than the fact he was super nice and easy to talk to. You realize you feel like you've known him forever! You wish you had suggested getting together another time, but you didn't think of it as you needed to hurry to your appointment. You don't have his number to be in touch, but you know where he likes to hang out. Rather than going there at random times to try and run into him as it would seem obvious as it isn't your usual hangout, you decide to take a few moments in quiet time and send him kind thoughts by expressing telepathically how lovely it was to meet and talk and you would love to have it happen again. You "send" the message you will be stopping by the coffee shop at 4pm the following day.

The next day you arrive there at 4pm. He isn't there but you buy a coffee and find a place to sit. Sipping your coffee, you look at the entrance and see him come in! He spots you and comes over to say hi. He asks you if it's OK if he joins you. He tells you he doesn't usually come in at this time but felt compelled to do so. He tells you he was so happy to see you there as he wanted to see you again and he regretted not asking you for your number. You exchange contact information and a new relationship unfolds.

This telepathic communication works for situations that are "meant to be". It feels very in sync like it's destiny to connect and be together. It's all to do with timing.

You will find that things like this happen more naturally as you become familiar and comfortable with it.

Sometimes telepathic communication happens when you are not trying.

Here is an example:

You get a call from someone you had thought about an hour before they called. It is a woman you worked with that you haven't heard from in a long time. She tells you she was thinking about you about an hour ago and thought she should give you a call to say hi when she finished what she was doing. You tell her you were thinking about her too!

Both find they have similar experiences happening in their lives so they can relate and give support to one another. Both have mothers with dementia and it's challenging dealing with them. Both have children leaving home to go to college in another city. Both have sudden relationship changes, one with divorce and the other with death.

They are both extremely happy to have connected and felt as if it was divine intervention. Sometimes things happen in mysterious ways to have people be in touch.

Connecting with Nature

Being in nature is one of the most effective and simple ways to tune in. It enhances your own energy, which in turn enhances your intuition. Becoming aware of the different frequencies and vibrations of nature is a great way to practise sensing energy and it helps to balance your own.

It depends on where you live as to what kind of landscapes and nature you can experience. Wherever it is, it's good for your soul!

If you have the opportunity to walk along a beach, be barefoot if you can to feel the sand and water on your feet. Breathe in the salty air and be aware of the feelings and sensations you have flowing throughout your body. Pick up some shells, pieces of wood and rocks and feel their energy. Choose a couple of them to take home so they can remind you of the way you felt at the beach. They help to ground you too; which means connecting to the Earth, to feel stable and secure. I myself have rocks in my car, in pockets and I keep a couple in my purse! You can also sit down on a log or on the rocks at the beach to absorb their energy as you look out at the ocean. Sense how it makes you feel.

Perhaps you live by a hillside or mountain where you can go hiking. When you do, stop to take time to sense your surroundings. Smell the fresh air and feel the earth or grass beneath your feet. Sit down on the rocks and feel their energy in your hands and throughout your body. Connect with the trees around you and absorb their vibrations. Be aware of how "grounded" and calm this makes you feel.

You may be lucky to live near a rainforest or a grove of trees that you can walk through. If so, try leaning against a tree and feel its vibration. Is it strong? Is it soft? Does it have a message for you? Sense and feel what its energy is like. Then go to another tree of a different kind and do the same. As you do this frequently, you will notice how different they are and it may surprise you what it has to say to you!

Maybe you live in a big city where there isn't very much nature. If you have a park nearby, just walking through the park and pausing to take in the energy will certainly do you some good. You may not be able to lean on trees, but you can stand near one or by flowers to experience their energy and take note of how it makes you feel.

Or perhaps you live in a desert where you can feel the vastness of the dry ground and unique plants and trees and the expansion of the endless sky.

You may be fortunate to live in lush tropical surroundings where flowers are abundant, fragrances heavenly and you have the opportunity to visit a beautiful waterfall. Once again, take note of these energies and how you feel being near them.

You can also experience the same thing with the beauty of a garden. Hold your hand up to a flower and sense its energy. You will be surprised from one flower to the next about how different they are; some are warm, some cool, some gentle, some strong. You can also do this with cut flowers too. When I do readings with a group of readers, I always have a vase of flowers on my table. I have experienced the energy of the flowers reaching out in front of me as I am doing the reading. It's like they were saying, "Tell her about us!" Even though they are cut flowers, they still have energy and vibrations.

Nature is the pure expression and manifestation of the Life Force Energy. You can learn much wisdom from nature. You can connect any time you want to—the more you practise, the more amazed you will be at what you sense and feel. Not only does it "ground" you, which means feeling connected to the Earth, it enhances your connection to your soul and intuition so you feel in balance. Being one with nature makes you realize you are made of the same energy as nature. We need to be grateful and respect and honour our connection.

If you are not in a position to be outdoors, you can make your connection even being indoors. Having plants and flowers adds positive energy and enhances the atmosphere. You may wish to collect pieces of wood or dried foliage to add to your surroundings. Also, if you can look out the window and see a tree, flowers, or the landscape, you can make a telepathic connection. This is a silent connection you can make by focusing with intention as you align your energy with the tree you are looking at. As you connect, sense how much better you feel.

The various seasons offer us a variety of experiences with nature. Depending on where you live, the energy of one season to another can be very different, yet in some places it doesn't vary much. It is interesting to take note of wherever you live as to which season resonates with you more than another. Or perhaps you love all of them equally as they offer you many different feelings and experiences. Do you feel happy in the spring, summer and fall, yet dread the winter? Or do you love the cold weather and snow of winter and find the heat of summer too much? It is interesting to see what resonates with you, as it tells you a lot about yourself!

A personal example:

I am very fortunate to live on Vancouver Island in British Columbia, Canada. I have access to beautiful beaches, lakes, rivers, waterfalls, forests, mountains, and valleys. I love to go to a forest by the ocean to sit amongst the beautiful "elders":

giant cedars, firs, maples, and pines. The energy of them makes me feel calm, peaceful and connected to ALL. I often lean against one of my favourite trees to feel their energy. As I do so, feeling "one" with the tree, I also say, "I release any energy that does not serve me for my highest good to be released to the tree to be transformed." I am always amazed at how wonderful I feel by doing this. I, too, remember to thank the trees for sharing their energy.

Connecting with Animals

Our dear animal souls are another way of practising using your intuition. Whether they be cats, dogs, fish, birds, hamsters, horses, donkeys—ALL animals are authentic and very aware. We can share giving them messages and interpreting their needs and vice versa. Ask your cat or dog to tell you something you need to hear. They communicate telepathically; you sense and feel what they are saying. Or look deeply into their eyes. Some try to communicate verbally. I myself have a little chihuahua that desperately tries to talk!

Animals are great teachers for us. Look at how intuitive and instinctive animals are. There are so many videos showing different animals caring for one another: horses snuggling baby ducks, dogs nursing newborn kittens that have lost their mother, cats adopting squirrels or monkeys, elephants consoling another elephant after the death of her partner—just to name a few. It appears they have got it right: acceptance of one another no matter what you look like, and being different from themselves. And not to forget mentioning how loyal and caring pets are to us humans!

I have a very extraordinary story for you. A client of mine loves fish. She and her husband built a fish pond in their backyard and filled it with goldfish. She loved her fish and the ambiance it brought to their garden. They had put in special filters to keep the water clean. One night she woke up from hearing her fish screaming to her telepathically! She was so alarmed, she went outside to see what was going on. She found the fish had been sucked up into the filter and had she not "heard" them so she could help, they all would have died. Now how amazing is that?

Creating Altars and Sacred Space

You may wish to create an "altar" in your place where you meditate or simply sit in silence. You can choose a few different objects you are attracted to such as certain coloured candles, rocks, shells, wood, feathers, crystals, statues such as angels, animal totems or something else that is meaningful to you. This creates an atmosphere for your own personal sanctuary. You are setting the energy for you to be able to feel relaxed and peaceful so you can tune in.

Books and Card Decks

You can also intuitively pick out some books to read that support you. Stand in front of the books in the bookstore and see which ones you find your hand moving towards. Before you open the book, ask for a message or say, "What is it I need to know?" and see what you find on the page you open it to. You may be pleasantly surprised there is a message/answer to a question you have been contemplating.

You may wish to check out books that have been recommended to you. Some people will tell you, "Oh, you must read this, it was so helpful to me," but it's best to check it out by looking through it while being open, and sensing if it resonates with you. Some you may find they do, while others not at all. This is where you use your intuition to feel if it is for you. Perhaps later on you will come across it again and it will feel right for you to read. Many people read eBooks now so you can't physically touch them to check them out, but you can certainly browse them to sense which one you may wish to read.

There are also many, many choices of cards such as tarot, oracle, mystical, archetypal, mythical, animal totems and fairy ones—to name a few—that you may be attracted to that you can learn about energy and yourself through the use of the cards. They show you different ways of using them with the book provided with the cards. You can certainly use their suggestions or you can simply play with them yourself by following your intuitive guidance. You may find yourself picking one out of the deck and learning about it for a day or two and how the choice fits into something that is happening in your life. Or you can open the book to a certain page that relates to one of the cards—so you find it in the deck and learn its meaning and how it correlates with something in your world.

Practices of Meditation, Yoga, and Physical Activity

Different practices of meditation, yoga and other physical exercises assist in becoming in tune with yourself on all levels. You may come across classes you are attracted to that you wish to take. There are many different options available to you. Perhaps you love to dance as it makes you feel free and it expresses who you are through your movement. There are a variety of meditation practices and various types of yoga. Choose ones that resonate with you that you feel *aligned* with. Some people enjoy more extreme physical exercise such as running, hiking, water sports, winter sports like snowboarding and skiing, or gym workouts that make their body, mind and spirit feel good.

It's fine to have people suggest things to you or recommend something, but the truth is, you need to *feel* if it is for you. When you are in tune, you will know!

A personal example for meditating:

When I first decided to look into what meditation was about, I came across a picture of the body showing the main chakras, which are the energy centres of the body. (There are many more chakras in the body besides the "main ones" or the more commonly known ones.) The main chakras correlate with the colours of the rainbow. Red is the root chakra at the base of the spine. Orange is the sacral chakra, between the navel and genitals. Yellow is the solar plexus chakra, above the navel below the chest. Green is the heart chakra, at the centre of the chest. Blue is the throat chakra, at the front of the neck. Indigo (purple/blue) is the third eye chakra, in the centre of the forehead, which represents intuition. Violet is the crown chakra, on top of the head.

I love colour so I decided to explore doing a meditation with the chakras. I started practising by envisioning the colour of each chakra, starting with the root chakra, moving from one chakra to another, until I reached the crown chakra at the top of the head. I took note of what I sensed about each one of them. Then I did the reverse, starting at the crown chakra, moving down through each chakra until I reached the root chakra.

At first I found it hard to quiet my mind and just focus on each chakra to feel its energy but I persevered, and eventually I found it easy to do. I definitely felt more balanced and calm. It was like doing a personal "tune up"! As I continued practising I noticed many different aspects of each chakra, and the various energies they represent in the body.

I did this each morning before I went to work. And I didn't do it in silence—I could hear traffic outside and various noises in my own place. It is suggested to meditate in a quiet setting but I didn't have the circumstances to do so. As I have mentioned, I have done readings for over twenty-five years in malls and various other venues. I needed to be able to tune in for people in a noisy setting. I look back at learning to meditate in noise, and now I see how valuable it is.

Remember, these are only tools to assist your unfoldment. You, yourself hold the wisdom you seek. The more you are aware and incorporate it in your life, the more it becomes natural. You suddenly realize you have this relationship within, knowing it is always there for you and it's like you have another "channel" you have connected to. When you realize your soul is connected to the Universal Energy by an invisible cord much like an umbilical cord, you know you have access to any information simply by this amazing fact. Every human on this planet has the capacity to access this information. It is our birthright—we just need to remember.

You may wish to keep a journal of your experiences as you practise the different suggestions. Doing so, you can see the progress you have made since starting.

Artistry, Expression, and Creativity

I have noticed with doing readings that many people do not think they are creative or artistic in any way. There are many forms of artistry through creativity, and they create your own unique expression of you, and who you are. Art isn't just about drawing and painting; it can be expressed in many ways. Being creative artistically can be expressed through cooking, gardening, painting, drawing, music, performing, singing, crafting, sewing, writing, sculpting, storytelling, poetry, reading, even by collecting objects or by offering certain services such as spa and beauty treatments (hair, nails), tattooing, and fashion. Anything you love to do and feel passionate about is an expression of who you are and teaches and tells you about yourself from your soul. It reveals your authentic you!

So, remember you have many gifts and talents that express who you are. By acknowledging this and giving it recognition you are honouring yourself. For those of you that don't feel creative, perhaps look into something that you are attracted to and give it a try! Let's say you've always wished you could paint animals. You could explore this by finding a class to get you started and you can continue experimenting on your own. It doesn't have to be professional and perfect; it can be a hobby. But you may find that you are better at it than you think you would be! This applies to other examples mentioned above. You may find that once you get going experimenting with your interests, it will open up different aspects of yourself and you will be motivated to explore even further!

Routines and Flexibility

Most people feel the need to have routines in their lives to keep it organized and together. When we are too rigid about following the routines though, it can create anxiety, especially when things don't go as you planned.

Sometimes we need to break routines in order to be more flexible. Being more "in the flow" also allows you to take note of and listen to your intuition.

Breaking routines is not meant to make you disorganized or undisciplined. It helps you to *sense* and *feel* what your spirit wants you to do in the moment. It also makes you more flexible and helps you not react when things don't go exactly as you planned.

Here are some suggestions to help you:

Try to not plan ahead with everything. Have some time in your day or a whole day where you plan nothing and allow yourself to be guided. Use your intuition to *sense* what to do. Perhaps you will feel like you wish to stay in your pyjamas and lie in bed, reading a book. Or you may sense you wish to go for a walk rather than vacuum like you usually would.

Don't get up/go to bed at usual times *every* day.

Pamper yourself to confirm love of self: treat yourself to something special, and make time for you. Have candlelight baths, your favourite food, or buy something special for yourself.

Break your day-to-day routines; choose to do things on different days.

Switch up your exercise routine and add something new.

Depending on your personality type, changing routines can be very challenging and uncomfortable. Try to remind yourself what your intention is by making these changes. You are doing so to help yourself to be open to listening to your inner voice—your intuition—and become familiar with its guidance. This creates flexibility and flow rather than being rigid with routines. What we are striving for in our lives is to integrate both physical and spirit, operating simultaneously.

Here is a personal example:

When my daughter was about three years old, I left my job in order to spend more time with her. I was used to having a routine to keep things in order due to my work. I had certain days I would do housework and certain days I would do shopping. My husband and I shared doing other chores. It felt very strange to not go to work. In fact, I found it very difficult due to having so much time being at home. I realized too that I didn't need to do things in the same way as I did when I was working, but I found it hard to break the routines I had set. So I purposely made myself not do housework and shopping in the same way I used to. I would take our daughter to the beach or to the park to play and leave my housework for another day. It felt very weird for me and I have to say I had some anxiety about it. But eventually I relaxed, and began to sense and feel when to do things, and found it was lovely to be spontaneous rather than be too strict with the routines I had created. I felt happier knowing I had a choice. I also found that I could blend and fit in what I needed to do to keep order in our lives and enjoy other things without feeling pressured or anxious. Everything seemed to flow in balance.

Sometimes unraveling routines can take you to the other extreme where you find you are becoming a little too loose with your days. If that's the case don't panic about it. Just be aware of it and then you can pay attention to bringing it back into balance.

Discernment and Advice

You can ask another's advice just to have a different viewpoint; however, it's important to check in with what is being said to you and *sense* if it *resonates* with you. What might be right for one person is not necessarily right for you. Once again, this is where your intuition comes into play. You can discuss situations with others and listen to their advice or their perspective, but if what they are saying does not feel right for you, then it isn't a fit for you. You may take certain parts of their advice and apply it in your own way, or perhaps it just doesn't resonate so you will choose to let go of it all.

Some people give out their advice when it hasn't been asked for. It is somewhat of a pattern or condition that they are used to in communicating and they perhaps don't even realize they do it. It is best to ask someone if they would like a suggestion or advice before handing it out, because then it doesn't come across as telling them what to do. This is a big problem in all different kinds of relationships!

Here is a personal example:

When I first began doing readings for people, one of the things that concerned me was I didn't want to tell people what to do. I wished to help and support them, but not make it that I knew what they should do as though my way was "the only right way". I found there was a very thin line there, and so it was very, very important for me to be discerning.

During that time I asked myself, "How do I make certain I am suggesting things rather than telling them?" I heard, "Say at the beginning that you wish for only the highest and best information to come through for them."

I also realized it was not up to me to *interpret* what the information I brought through meant—unless the client asked me, or they wished to hear my viewpoint. When I sense to say something, I ask them first if I may make a suggestion. By doing this, I feel I am honouring them, the information coming through, as well as myself. It is being respectful of all concerned.

It is best for us all to remember to be mindful and discerning in the way we communicate and in giving suggestions and advice. I truly don't think that many people like being told what to do and how to do it!

Intuition and Timing

You often hear people say, "I was in the right place at the right time." Everything IS about timing, which is one of these oxymorons or contradictions we find in our world: We have to be mindful of time, all the time. Be on time, find time to do things, pay things on time, make time—yet the truth is, *there is no time* except what we as humans have made!

It IS all about timing, though! And this is where your intuition and instinct come into play.

When you are paying attention to your intuition, your instinct and timing, then you are "riding the wave of time" and this is when things just seem to flow and fall into place and the timing is perfect.

When things flow and fall into place, it happens when you are not trying to control the timing and the way it is opening up for you. You are trusting things will come together when they are meant to. Perfect timing is when all the threads of energy weave together magically!

Riding the Wave of Time

There are times when you feel everything is aligned and ready to go, yet all of a sudden it feels like the brakes have been put on or there is a block stopping you from having things move forth smoothly. Then everything is backed up and you try and figure out why nothing is falling into place like it felt it was going to. But you then know it isn't the perfect time for all to align and come together and it is out of your control.

There are many factors that come into play with this, one being astrological influences. Many are aware that during full moons there can be disruptions and heightened emotions.

This, too, is true when different planets are in retrograde; for instance, when Mercury is in retrograde there are communication glitches, delays and disruptions of various kinds. This happens also when certain planets are in different configurations. All we can do is be aware of this as we have no control. Then all of a sudden, as if someone has taken the plug out of the dam, everything seems to go forward and all falls into place nicely after all. It helps us to know these things to function in our 3D world!

There are a lot of factors that are at play and part of our timing every day. This is why it is so important to be connected to your intuition and to be flexible, as things can change in a heartbeat. When you understand this, you are freeing yourself up from being upset that something hasn't happened in the time frame you wanted it to. You are accepting of the delay or change and you keep "your antennas" alert to receive the guidance and perfect timing when things are meant to move forth. This is also true when you ask a question and you don't get an answer; the time is not right to know.

Here is a perfect example of "Riding the Wave of Time":

As I have mentioned, I have done readings in various settings such as malls over many years. In 2018 I was invited to do readings at a mall where I live. Between four readers, we needed to cover eight weeks, seven days a week, having two readers available. I committed to do three weeks out of the eight weeks. I was a little hesitant about it, as I am not really fond of the mall atmosphere; however, I love doing readings. At that time, I found myself saying, "OK Universe, if I commit to sitting in a mall, I'll make you a deal. I would love to meet someone aligned with me that can help me with my writing." I had been writing a couple of different books for some time, but was yet to meet someone that I felt aligned to work with.

On one of my weeks off, I received a phone call to ask me if I was interested in doing another week, as one of the readers was not able to do it after all. I found myself saying, "Sure, I'll do it." During that week I had a young woman come to me for a reading. As she sat down in front of me, I felt an instant connection with her. I began the reading and much information came forth about her gifts and talents, one being writing. At the end of the session, she shared with me that she enjoyed and appreciated the reading, and she handed me a business card. Her company is called "The Awakened Press". I had a huge flow of energy rush through my body! I thanked her and we both said let's stay in touch.

At the end of that day, I looked up "The Awakened Press" website to see what it was about. Lindsay was the Editor In Chief of the company. "Oh, my God!" I thought. "My wish has been answered! I met my person who can help me with my writing!"

I connected with Lindsay, and we started working together. As we did so, more was revealed about the AMAZING TIMING of us connecting. First of all, I was not originally supposed to be at the mall the day we met—I was filling in for someone. When I told Lindsay that, she told me that she wasn't really meant to be in the mall either. She had rented a car and needed to return it to a place in the downstairs of the mall. She had spent a couple of hours having to deal with a problem with returning the car, but instead of leaving to continue on where she was going next, she decided to come upstairs in the mall and just sit on a bench to chill out for a bit after the exhausting ordeal with the car. She said she was feeling a little down and doubtful about her life at that time, and was reflecting on all as she was sitting there. And while she was sitting there contemplating, she was asking for guidance about what to do with her life next, and asking whether or not she was on the right track. All of a sudden she heard a voice say to her, "Look up." She looked up and to her awe and amazement there was a giant banner attached to the railing above that said "Psychic Circle: Tarot, Intuitive Readings". Lindsay was so surprised she quickly got up and took the escalator to the floor above and landed in front of the booth offering the readings. She saw me, and instantly knew she was meant to come and have a reading.

And here we are! Lindsay and I began working together on this book. She received confirmation from the reading that her business is on track and totally aligned with what she is meant to offer. And my wish came true by meeting someone who I'm aligned with that can help me with my writing! Magical, perfect, illogical timing!!

Lindsay and I did not know about the perfect synchronicity of our timing until we actually started working together two years later. We then shared stories and learned about our unique experiences while in the flow of the divine timing.

This is why when you are open to your intuition and hearing the voice from within, you are automatically "Riding the Wave of Time" because you are operating from your inner guidance.

So, just remember to pause for a few minutes before you react when things seem to not be going the way you thought they would. Your mind had the plan, but your intuition knows there is more to it than "the plan". It's timing! So if you remind yourself of that, then you save yourself from reacting with disappointment, anger and frustration, as you know there are other reasons/factors involved and eventually the timing will be perfect. This reminder also helps you to be more in the moment and present, which is truly what time is!

Energy

Everything is energy; therefore you are affected by energy all the time. It is important to recognize this so you can manage your own energy, so you can decipher and be aware of what is happening around you, and still have a clear connection to your intuition.

Remember in the first section I mentioned our *essence self*— our soul—is energy? Our physical body is energy too, so it is important to keep clearing our "circuits" in our body so we can function in balance with our body/mind and spirit/soul, in synergetic orchestration.

Clearing Your Circuits

During your life, you accumulate so many various experiences that remain within your being.

As you are energy yourself, much of the information or experiences you hold within your circuits is old, that has no use to you any longer, or perhaps never did—and it is literally clogging your lines. It is most important to *clear your circuits* so you can have clear communication or to have a *direct line* to your intuition. It is necessary to *release energy that does not serve you*. It is like clearing your desktop on your computer, and emptying the contents you don't need anymore into the trash! This clearing also allows you to be able to tune in to other energies around you, to your loved ones or to events that are happening in the world.

Here is an example:

You get up in the morning after having a wonderful sleep. You make your coffee and take it to your usual comfortable chair by the window overlooking your garden. As you are sitting there, simply enjoying your coffee, you suddenly have a wave or sense of despair. Since you have been practising clearing your circuits and listening to your intuition, you pause and take a few minutes to tune in and sense the energy you are picking up on. You firstly check in to sense if it is something to do with yourself or your loved ones. Your intuition tells you, "No, it's none of you, all are well." You then check in to sense if it is something going on in the world, and you sense, "Yes, it is." You now know it is something "out there" and not something in your own life. You decide after enjoying the rest of your coffee to check the news to back up what you are feeling and find out there has been a terrorist attack in Europe where many innocent people were killed.

This example shows how being able to sense energy is not always happy news. But it shows you how you can tune in and rely on your intuition to notify you of what's happening not only in your own life, but for others, too. By being able to tune in to your other channel—your intuition—you are able to "know" certain things beyond logic and practical, physical ways. Of course it's best to be able to tune in to the lighter, brighter things in life!

Here is another example on the lighter side:

You are going about your day as usual and as you are driving along to go grocery shopping you suddenly get an overwhelming feeling of excitement. Even though you are driving and having to keep your focus, you ask yourself what this feeling is about. You instantly get the vision of your sister, who is on a holiday in Hawaii. Thinking it may just be that you are picking up on that she must be having a lovely time, you sense, "It's more than that." After you do your shopping and you are putting your groceries in the car, your phone rings and it is your sister. Enthusiastically, you answer. Her voice is full of excitement, and you tell her that you were sensing her. She says, "I don't doubt that." Guess what? She tells you that she was having lunch with a friend at a restaurant on the beach where they were filming a movie, and she was approached by a director who asked her if she would like to be in the movie! He said she has the exact look they were wanting!

How to Release Energy

We have all had experiences in our lives where we have been led to believe something is the truth, or it feels as if we have been programmed to think a certain way, when it is not serving us for our highest good. Due to this, it is important for us to clear our energy.

Releasing energy and clearing programs is extremely effective in helping to connect to your intuition. It takes time and discipline, so you have to have patience! But you will find how miraculous this can be for you when you start practising these techniques. What is important is to not be too hard on yourself. Some experiences are easy to release, whereas others can be like breaking through cement. It can take time to dissolve and clear, yet it may happen faster than you think. Everyone is different depending on his or her personal circumstances.

These techniques mentioned may accompany conventional counselling or traditional practices such as shamanistic, due to deep traumas and abuse.

To release energy that does not serve you, I suggest this:

Choose a quiet place indoors or a secluded place outdoors where you can relax, sitting in a comfortable position. You may wish to have a "sacred space" where you do this, such as you would in meditating. You could light a candle, use sage to cleanse the space, or have other objects you love or are connected to (such as rocks, crystals, feathers, or statues) to enhance and support your experience.

Take three deep breaths, breathing in through your nose and out through your mouth. Say out loud or in your mind, "I release any energy that does not serve me for my highest good from my physical body." You may have sensations come up such as a jerking or twitching motion in your body where you are releasing a block, pain, or discomfort. You may find yourself standing up to shake or move your body to release energy. Take your time while doing this; you may wish to pause or repeat the process.

Next say, "I release any energy that does not serve me for my highest good from my mental body." You may recall memories or thought forms that appear as they are clearing and deleting. Just let them go. Some people have visions or memories of experiences that show up, whereas others do not; they just feel the release as a sensation. Try to detach from any images that come to you, as the mind may want to attach to them or the story that goes with them. If you find that you have some disturbing memories or visions, perhaps go slowly with this so you are not overwhelmed. *You are not doing this to recall and review the experience, you are doing so to clear and have it removed from your mind.* Just take your time and be kind to yourself as you go along with the process.

Then say, "I release any energy that does not serve me for my highest good from my emotional body." Emotions may come up where you can blow them out or even verbally release with a scream or some other sound, or you may burst into tears. It is simply letting go and clearing. You may wish to stand up to move your body with the releasing. This experience can also be overwhelming depending on the emotions that surface. Take your time and remember if it is too much at first, just go slowly and allow yourself to tell you if it is too much.

And lastly, "I release any energy that does not serve me for my highest good from my spiritual body." Perhaps we have spiritual beliefs we carry that no longer serve us or perhaps never did.

When you feel you have completed the techniques for the time being, you may wish to end the session with stretching your body as you feel the need to. Do this intuitively by letting your body show you where it wishes to move. Perhaps it will wish to shake your limbs and torso, then your head to complete releasing energy. Or it may move as if dancing with a gentle flow. Or you may stretch in various stances that are also completing the releasing.

End it by standing tall with your feet slightly apart for balance and hold your hands together (as if in prayer), reaching just above your head. Then move them slowly down in front of you by your heart, then move them slowly to your waist and open up your hands, moving them out in front of you with a motion of gratitude as you continue to open your arms out to your sides…then lower your arms to your side. Bow your head forward in closing if it feels right to you.

I suggest practising this clearing technique daily to become familiar with the process. It may not feel necessary to do so in the future when you are noticing a positive difference in yourself from doing it daily. However, doing it every couple of days will help you to be clear. You may choose to do it in the shower, having the water help wash away and cleanse your energy. Or do it simply with intention as you sit in silence by yourself.

Here is a personal example:

I find I like to do the clearing techniques in the bath as water is a conductor of energy. Before I begin I say, "I align, I attune to Source, the energy of All That Is, that of love, that of light, that of the divine. As I do so I release any energy that does not serve me for my highest good to be given back to Source to be transformed. I acknowledge each; physical, mental, emotional and spiritual bodies."

I take this time to acknowledge my body and thank it for housing my spirit. I acknowledge what an amazing intricate body that it is and I say certain things such as, "I know all parts of my body operate in balance simultaneously with perfect orchestration." I also go into more detail, such as saying, "All the trillions of cells in my body communicate with love and light."

I also find myself saying, "I release, I let go, I surrender," throughout my day. As you are "out there" going through the different experiences you have during the day, you can pick up energies you may not wish to keep. It truly helps to do these clearings often.

If you choose to do these clearings outdoors, you can also have nature help you cleanse. You can lean against a tree and release energy that does not serve you, giving it to the tree to be transformed or release it into the ground.

If there are specific situations or feelings you particularly know you wish to release, say them out loud or do so in your mind. These can be fears, emotions, or memories of unpleasant scenes. Sometimes you have to do this practice over and over again until you sense they are released. It is like "emptying the trash" and clearing programs on your computer. You will feel lighter and brighter on all levels, physically, mentally, emotionally, and spiritually!

Here is another example:

You recall being at school where you experienced a number of different teachers telling you that you will get nowhere in life, due to not paying attention. Them telling you this has burdened you throughout your life and triggered you at different times when you were trying to get a job or coming up with innovative ideas, even in your relationships. You were not completely aware of how deeply their statements affected your self-esteem.

You decide it is time to let go of these words and judgments as you know deep down they are not true and you wish to rid yourself of them for good.

You practise doing the releasing technique by stating you let go of all the statements the teachers said to you about never getting anywhere in life. You picture all of the words deleting from your mind and dissolving from your whole being. You find you feel them sort of leaving, but you sense a couple of the statements are still with you. You continue to practise deleting them on a daily basis. You find that each time you do the process, it becomes simpler and quicker and more effective. You also realize how it has affected your physical body, as when you have released the statements from your mind, you feel your body relax and find you feel an inner energy emerging that feels very present and powerful! You then realize you have been holding back on showing your true self, due to the image you carried of yourself not getting anywhere in life, because of the comments made. Realizing this and seeing how much lighter and brighter you feel, you become very confident about all aspects of your life and you watch yourself changing and becoming very successful, sharing your gifts and talents and having meaningful relationships that you feel comfortable with. You feel very happy and content within yourself.

Toning and Sound

Another way of clearing your circuits as well as "tuning up" your body, which in turn helps you tune in to your intuition, is by toning.

As we are energy, different vibrations and frequencies have an effect on us. It is proven scientifically that this is true. Toning is sounding and holding different sounds and notes. I have experimented with this alone and in groups, and it is astounding how you feel when you do this!

A simple thing to do is to hum with your mouth closed. Apparently, it actually gives your brain a "tune up". When I tried this, I was quite amazed at how alert I felt.

Also, there is much information available about sound therapy. It is known that certain vibrations and frequencies create healing.

So, you may wish to explore toning and sound. It not only clears, it enhances your energy and your intuition.

How Does Energy Affect You?

As we now know, everyone and everything is energy that has different vibrations and frequencies. Knowing and acknowledging this makes you realize how much you are affected by the atmosphere and who and what you are around.

Some energies you resonate with, whereas others you do not. It is best to choose to be around supportive, positive, heightened energy (people, situations) when you can, rather than those that are low energy (manipulative, controlling, complaining, and focusing on what is wrong/doesn't work). I often describe it to clients by relating it to TV and radio waves. Some people are on the AM station, some FM, and some are on High Definition and beyond.

Of course, it is not always possible to discern what is going on in the energy field we are in. If you are a sensitive person, you can be highly affected by the energy you are around. Even those that do not perceive themselves as sensitive can be affected in not a nice way. This simple fact helps you really get to see who you are and how you operate. This can be challenging at times as you sometimes feel you have to be around people you may not want to be with, such as family or work situations. Sometimes your buttons get pushed or you get triggered by comments and your emotions show up, leaving you in a position where there is a reaction in a defensive or negative way. You then wish you had simply let it go and not reacted.

This is when it is helpful to know how to and practise "to detach" from the energy created so you can let it go and not react. It is changing your perception of it by "observing" and then detaching from emotions/reactions of the situation. You may need to go off to be alone somewhere for a couple of minutes to have time to remind yourself that you are not going to react, you are going to detach. The more you do so and are conscious of detaching, the easier it will become. It is better if you are able to simply remove yourself so you are not affected by the energy; but as mentioned before, this is not always possible.

Make certain your *intention* with *any exchange of energy* is for the highest and best of all concerned. Using it "out of alignment" is manipulation, which is a very low vibration.

"Whatever Frequency You Align to Becomes Your Reality"

What does that mean? Let me explain. For instance, if you always pay attention to what is wrong in the world, that becomes your reality. Perhaps you have a habit of watching the news a few times a day. It can be an obsession. A lot of what is on the news is disturbing and negative, letting us know all the things going on in the world that are not so great. You are being "fed" this disturbing energy; therefore, you can be deeply affected without even realizing you are. That is the frequency you have aligned to. This can affect your emotions, your physical body, and your mental state. You may become a worrier and perhaps you are very sensitive, so you can be highly affected by what you hear that isn't good for your well--being.

Let's turn the coin. You make a conscious choice to be positive and connect with uplifting people and situations. You may tune in to the news or read about what's happening in the world but you do so just to keep up to date. You are disturbed by what you hear, but you "detach" and you feel perhaps you might contribute to solutions, if you can. However, you don't allow it to "feed" you that energy, as you try to remain as positive and hopeful as you can. So this positive frequency that you align to, is your reality.

Managing and Protecting Your Energy

When your energy is clear, as we discussed earlier about clearing your circuits, and you can protect your clear energy, it definitely helps in being able to hear your inner voice, your intuition.

Here is an example:

All colours have a different frequency.

Tuning in to a colour you love or feel comforted by is very effective in protecting your energy. Let's take purple, for instance. Picture yourself being in an "egg" of beautiful purple. Make certain you are surrounded by the colour, from the inside out glowing all around you. This creates a "buffer zone", helping you harbour your own energy, and at the same time it helps you to not absorb energy you may not want. I often tell people to do this when you have to go into places with lots of mixed energy, such as a mall. Malls have such a jumble of energies, from the lights, sounds and lots of people that feel very static and prickly. It can disrupt your own energy. By practising this technique often, it will assist you in your efforts to sense and feel, by tuning in to a colour that feels right for you in the moment. You will find it varies from day to day; just tune in and ask yourself what colour would be good for today and see what colour comes to your mind. Doing this helps you to be able to be in the energy but you can still hear your inner voice, as you have protected your own energy by being in the egg of colour and not have the "atmosphere energy" affect you.

I'd like to share a personal experience with you. I have mentioned that I have done readings with a group of readers at various malls. I was invited to join them for a week at a time, a few times during the year. I heard my inner voice say, "Do them, say yes!" I was quite taken aback by how strongly my inner voice was telling me to join them, as I don't like malls. I was hesitant to, wondering how I could possibly do a reading in such an unlikely atmosphere full of static energy, noise, and so many people. But I found myself accepting the offer and surprised myself that I was able to tune in for people despite the atmosphere. It was a definite practice for me to learn the art of being able to tune out what was going on around me and be fully present with my client to tune in. It was like we created a bubble around us all so we could do the reading—and the client was able to receive without being affected by the atmosphere too. I ended up doing these readings for about twenty years and I actually enjoyed it, as I met so many interesting people from all over the world! It also conditioned me to be able to tune in anywhere, despite noise, distractions, and lots of people. It has been an exceptionally valuable experience that I didn't realize how much so when I accepted the offer.

As I have said before, you don't often know why you do things until much later on. That's why it is so important to listen to our inner voice. All experiences are precious threads woven into the tapestry of your own unique life.

Intuition, Energy, and Beyond

Heightening and fine-tuning your energy enhances your intuition. It is like moving your energy from an AM to FM radio station to High Definition and beyond! The more you do so, you will begin to have some amazing experiences that take you to another level. The levels are endless! It is exciting, inspirational, and it makes your life much more fulfilled.

You feel like you live here on Earth, yet you have the ability to connect with the cosmos and other dimensions through the connection to your soul. You truly know and feel you are not alone and there is much, much more to existence than here. The key to it is to always hold the intention that you are open to receive messages for "the highest and best for all concerned." By recognizing this, your experiences are positive. This also makes you realize that we are visitors on Earth to contribute our gifts to the experience.

As you experience and trust your intuition more and more, you gain a sense of belonging, fulfillment, and a sense of knowing beyond this realm. You gain self-confidence, self--acceptance and self-love. You know you are beautiful and worthy and have many unique gifts and talents to share and contribute in this life.

You realize that by being in tune with your own soul and beyond, it is contributing to the greater whole—not just in your own life, but it makes a difference to the existence of everyone on planet Earth, as well as planet Earth herself. In other words, how you live your life affects ALL.

You also have a deep sense of purpose. All relationships and perceptions in your life begin to take on a different meaning. You can sense and see why you've done what you've done in your life, revealing the patterns of your own majestic tapestry. You sense love, and you feel compelled to share love, as you realize that is what you are.

Connecting to Beyond

Many people find it difficult to quiet their mind of thoughts. I have experimented with this, and I will share something I found effective in quieting my mind so I can tune in.

I speak to my mind by saying, "I love you and I am grateful for you but I don't need you right now, so you can have time out. I will let you know when I need you again." When I did this, I found my mind felt relieved! It came to me to picture my mind in a beautiful yellow "box" where it can rest. You may wish to try this.

When you quiet your mind to be open to receiving messages from Spirit, you make a stronger connection with your true essence, which in turn connects you beyond this Earth plane. To do so, picture yourself as transparent (clear and empty). Welcome new frequencies to enter your being that serve you for your highest good. As you do this regularly, you will feel the sensation of "being upgraded". The energy feels heightened, charged. You may have visions in your mind's eye of a Spirit Guide or an energy form, or perhaps just a colour. You may simply hear a voice/message from a loved one in the Spirit World. You may not have visions or messages, you may just feel accelerated energy or a sense of well-being, which is perfectly fine. Again, the more you practise this consistently, the more experiences you will have.

Here is an example:

When I first started to try and relax and welcome new frequencies, I felt a rush or charged energy within myself. As mentioned, it is a sensation of being "upgraded". After sensing this, I then heard a voice say to me to go and get a pen and paper. I was surprised yet excited. I sat down and had a lovely transmission come through that was telling me about the spirit world and other dimensions. It was a very lovely energy, not the least bit scary. I continued having these messages come through to me often.

If you don't receive visions or messages at first, you are not doing something wrong. Everyone is different in the time it takes to be open and clear to receive. Have patience and be kind to yourself. And remember to always say at the beginning, "I only welcome energies that serve me for my highest good and I ask for divine protection." Doing this aligns you to benevolent energy so you need not feel afraid to connect to beyond.

As it becomes familiar to you in receiving messages and visions, it can also happen to you when you are simply doing something mundane or not trying to. You may suddenly feel the urge to look up and above you see a beautiful eagle or hawk flying by. Or you are standing in your yard and suddenly hear a voice say, "Look down," and there is a gift from Spirit; a tiny hummingbird feather. Or you are driving along the road listening to the radio and a song comes on that reminds you of spending time with your grandfather who is now in the Spirit World. These are just a few examples. Spirit speaks to us in miraculous ways!

Here is a personal example:

I was in my kitchen washing dishes. As I was rinsing one of them, I heard a voice say, "Look out the window." Startled, I looked outside where it had been snowing heavily all day (it was unusual to have this happen where I live). I stared out at the backyard that was a blanket of fresh snow. I didn't see anything that stood out to me, so I continued to wash the dishes. I then heard, "Look in the window sill." It seemed strange to me to hear this as the window sill was filled with snow that had blown in with the wind. I leaned over the sink to try and see the outside window sill and there, lying on top of the snow was a very tiny hummingbird feather! I couldn't believe it. How could such a tiny feather land and stay there in the wind and snow? It looked like it had been placed there for me to see. We did have a hummingbird feeder in the window, but the sweet nectar had frozen during the unusual cold weather, so we had not seen hummingbirds in days. As I looked at the feather, I felt the presence of my father who is in the Spirit World. Hummingbirds seem to be a symbol of my father's presence. I had been concerned about something going on in my life and I realized as I looked at the feather, it was there from my father to tell me not to worry, that things will be OK. And he was right—it all sorted itself out just fine! By the way, I managed to retrieve that sweet little feather after much time trying to get the frozen window open and do so before the feather blew away!

When you begin to have these experiences of "Spirit speaking to you", you may not be sure of who or what the symbol means for you. It is different for everyone, yet there are some guidelines you may wish to learn from various teachings. For instance, a hawk is a messenger in some cultures. So, when I see a hawk, I feel I am being alerted that I am receiving a message so to be aware of what that might be. When I see hummingbirds I feel it is my father, and when I find white feathers I know it is a friend in the Spirit World connecting with me. I suggest asking yourself "who or what is this symbol meaning for me" and see what first comes to your mind. You may instantly feel the presence of a loved one in the Spirit World, or you may see an eagle and feel it means a change for the better is coming in your life. It is actually fun and inspiring to interpret them for yourself.

"Put the Ego in Its Place and Allow Your Spirit to Guide You"

Be aware of the following facts:

Ego resists change;
spirit welcomes change, as it knows it is growth.

Ego likes to control and manipulate;
spirit gently guides with flow.

Ego likes to plan and have a routine;
spirit is spontaneous, guiding in the moment.

Ego looks for external power and outside recognition;
spirit humbly glows from within, it is an internal silent power.

Mindful Words

Align and attune (I *align* and attune to the Source)

Love rather than want (I'd *love* a wonderful relationship)

Welcome rather than want (I *welcome* new beginnings)

Sense and feel rather than think (I *sense* or *feel* this is the right thing to do); *sensing IS believing!*

Detach: removes you from emotional reactions (I *detach* from the energy)

Synchronicities (acknowledge *synchronicities* rather than seeing them as coincidences)

Vibrations, Frequencies, Resonance: relates to energy

Declarations

You may have heard of "affirmations" which are statements "affirming" something such as, "My day will be joyful and peaceful." I have practised affirmations during my exploring; however, I felt something was missing. It didn't feel like it was coming from within myself. So I tuned in to see what I could do to feel right for myself. I suddenly heard, "Declare it." That felt right to me! So I wrote a number of "declarations" that I would read throughout my day and I found they felt solid as I declared them. I read them out loud at first so I could really feel the statements.

The following declarations are some examples. You may wish to create some of your own.

"I look forward to each day with enthusiasm, finding pleasure in my encounters. I accept all disruptions with good humour."
THUS IT IS DECLARED SO IT SHALL BE, INDEED

"I allow myself to receive pure love, the pulse of the Universe. I graciously accept through my heart. I attune to this loving frequency in alignment with my purpose."
THUS IT IS DECLARED SO IT SHALL BE, INDEED

"I have courage to speak my truth with great confidence. I speak from my heart with integrity, allowing my intuition to choose my words. My intention is to have supportive, peaceful, inspirational communications."
THUS IT IS DECLARED SO IT SHALL BE, INDEED

"I create the vision I wish my life to be in alignment with my intuitive guidance. As the Universe is limitless, I know my resources are limitless, expanding my awareness."

THUS IT IS DECLARED SO IT SHALL BE, INDEED

"I have primal trust to live my life to the fullest, knowing I am safe and stable to do so. I have courage to be fully rooted in who I am, and I know all my needs will be met."

THUS IT IS DECLARED SO IT SHALL BE, INDEED

Here is a saying that you may wish to read or say out loud throughout your day, or perhaps first thing in the morning before you begin your day:

"With love and grace, I acknowledge my core essence, my true self; my soul, my spirit. I accept this vibration of authenticity with honour, dignity and respect. I know by listening to my soul's voice, my intuition, I am guided in my life and all my needs are met for my evolution. Knowing my soul is one with Source, brings me strength, clarity, truth, and FREEDOM!

And so be it."

"Believe in Yourself and You'll See Who You Are!"

About the Author

Maureen Freeman, Intuitive Advisor, Medium, and Channel, also known as Sage. In ancient times a Sage was a messenger/teacher delivering profound insights to those seeking counsel. For over 25 years, Maureen has been providing support to people with her natural psychic gifts. She has done thousands of readings, hundreds of channelings, taught classes on developing one's psychic abilities, interviewed on TV and radio, and lectured at Health Expos and other events. She has written columns and articles for various magazines and journals. She sees herself as a messenger delivering what is the highest and best for her clients. She lives in Victoria, British Columbia, Canada with her husband, one daughter, a grandson and a number of four-legged loved ones.

"My passion is supporting others with the gifts I have been graced with." —Maureen

Find out more at:

www.amessengersmessage.com